I AM NOT MYSELF TODAY

I AM NOT MYSELF TODAY

Poems

By Jill Haber Pallone

I am Not Myself Today
©2019 Jill Haber Pallone
ISBN: 978-0-578-58082-1

Cover Image: "Double Portrait of the Artist in Time," by Helen Lundeberg (1935). Used with kind permission of the Smithsonian American Art Museum, which reserves all rights to reproduction.

Front and back cover design courtesy of Camille Buch, of Buch Design. www.buchdesignandillustration.com

Dedicated to my beloved husband, Bob.
"The world is not the same."

Acknowledgments

Many thanks to the loving, faithful friends who have always encouraged my writing. Special thanks to lifelong friend Mimi Burstein, a most attentive and perceptive reader, whom I can always count on for honesty and support.

And to Dr. Gretta Leopold, whose patience, wisdom, and compassion helped me to become myself.

CONTENTS

Dedication

Acknowledgments

Introduction

POEMS

Introduction

I am pleased and honored to offer this short introduction to Jill's first published collection of poems, most of which have been selected from her work over the last five years. As her husband and best friend, I am glad for the opportunity to contribute to this project. As her greatest admirer, among many, I am excited to introduce her finely crafted and layered art to new readers.

It has been argued that some of the best art derives from adversity, or rather, the artist's personal response to moments of adversity. Jill's life story includes many such moments, and she has spent a large part of her life, and our life together these last 36 years, searching out creative ways to process, understand, and integrate them with an evolving and often uncertain sense of her own self.

She grew up in Philadelphia, a child of the fifties and sixties, terrified of nuclear annihilation in a family in which the parents were not always equipped to deal with anxiety, whether their children's or their own. She studied English and writing (and learned to play the sitar!), at the University of Pennsylvania, where her father was a professor, and where she became a favorite student, and later a long-time friend, of the novelist, Philip Roth.

After graduating from Penn, she joined Stanford's creative writing graduate program, but soon after abandoned it when her mounting emotional vulnerabilities became inextricably manifested in a paralyzing fear of earthquakes.

The next decade was a roller coaster ride; she finished two master's degrees back at Penn, while also being treated for a frightening emotional illness that sometimes brought her, in her words, "to the doors of madness" and prompted an attempt at suicide. After years of struggle, including several hospitalizations, she came under the care of a gifted doctor who helped her regain much of what she feared was lost forever. But the challenges didn't stop: a lost baby; severe depression; and the overwhelming pressures of a stressful writing/editing job, where her own voice was submerged. These were accompanied by the ever-present fear of again losing her balance and drifting off center. In the poem "Crossing Borders," she describes it:

> It can be
> distressing,
> this shifting
> ground—
>
> things are not
> where they were,

all markers
are torn
down.

While facing these challenges, Jill has always kept
writing; it is integral to her healing. Even a cursory
reading of the poems in this collection reveals that they
are often intensely personal. Some are difficult to read,
for she lays bare intense pain and sadness; others are
joyful, capturing the pleasures of a light breeze, the
warmth of the sun, the companionship of a friend, and
the infinite love that arises from creating a shared life
with another. That love, and the melding of our two
souls, is the driving force for the most joyful poems in
this collection, such as this one:

Mutual Creation

How lovely they are—
the blood-red pepper,
the onion and corn,
simmering in the pan,
like stained glass lit
by fire.

You throw back your head
and laugh
as you crack an egg

against the side
of a bowl
and watch it slide
to the bottom,

and I lean in towards you
to reach a wooden
spoon.

Seamlessly sharing steps
like seasoned dancers,

we are building something new
from disparate pieces,

chopping, mixing, spreading
till it rises
to become itself—

our mutual creation.

More careful reading reveals that Jill's language, while
spare and light, nonetheless flows thick with meaning.
Hers is a gentle voice in your ear, proposing a glance in
the direction of an observed or sensed reality. Her tools
are simple, yet well chosen for digging down and
uncovering, laying out exquisite subsoil. She leaves to
others the grand parades of history and machinations
of the political mind, preferring instead to shine her

light on the heart in its hours of pain, joy, hope, and wide-mouthed disbelief. In doing so, she seeks to create a well-lit image, which reflects her essential truths.

I hope that you, her new readers, will find your own truths in these poems as well.

Robert L. Pallone
Lugano, Switzerland
10 September 2019

POEMS

Let's

Let's fly
together,
pale moths
to winter
light.

Let's fall
together,
deep into the sea,
mingling stardust
far beneath
the waves.

Let's climb
together
in the lifeblood
of a tree,
drinking in the essence
of the sun.

Let's do just

as we've imagined,
as we've always
done.

The Physics of Love

Over mussels
and wine
you told me of
particles

that even a universe
apart
are as entangled

as a mother
and her unborn
child.

We ate and drank
and spoke of the impossibly
possible

as we never had before.

Then the music drew us up

and we danced and we
danced and we
danced, wrapped
tight
in each other's
arms

till we blended
together,
solid
as the earth,
mysterious as space
and time.

April

It tastes

like a tickle
in my belly,

too fleeting to speak
of—

a memory
of a memory,

sweet,
and pink as tongues,

white
as falling ash.

When I try
to sing,
its sound
eludes me

though I feel
that once

I knew
it well

and I still
can hear it vaguely,
everywhere.

April
is a painful
kindness—

a soft, elderly
hand

on my small
head

pressing gently

just before
I sleep.

Shiva

There is a song
in you—
a sound
of sympathetic
strings

spreading slowly
into silent
skies.

Though you have seen
this world
before,
you are jarred
by its right
angles
and sudden
turns.

They spin you

toward darkness
till you are all
alone

and must repair
your ancient
soul
with the cool,
hard stones
of rest
and reason.

Then the song
begins
to return,
and you listen—

eyes clear and wide,
waiting wisely
for the joy
of resolution.

In Old Dubai

She reached out
her hand
as I stepped into
the wooden
boat.

I took it
with the gratitude
of women reaching

over water,
reaching over
broken glass,
reaching past
the trespasses
of men.

She smiled
and I smiled at her,
wanting to stay close

to her, breathe in
the ether
of her life.

But instead I crossed
to the other
side
as the boat swayed
slowly
through the muddy
creek

and she
and her sisters,
wrapped in the ghostly
mystery
of their dark
robes,

sat secure
in their intimate
history
of flesh and blood.

Solitaire

The things left unsaid
overwhelm me
as you deal yourself
the Jack, the Queen,
hoping for the neat,
improbable closure
of a winning hand.

If you end it cleanly,
you will stop
and look around
at the empty room

feeling the blankness
one feels when a book
is finally closed
and in your hands
you hold the inscrutable
flatness
of its cover.

If the cards defy you,
leaving ends untied,
you may breathe more easily,
knowing that your next step
is to try again.

Time passes slowly
as you fill your hours
with these familiar faces.
The King is always welcome,
the Ace brings a smile.

But I am saddened
as I watch you.
Time is clearly against us
as your memory dims
and your hair thins
and your sweetness grows
ever sweeter.

I want to speak
the unspeakable
as I kiss your cheek

on my way out the door—

to tell you that
your daughter loves you
and wants you never to go.

And I try to find ways
to show you
how the world
will be cruel
without you
without breaking both
our hearts.

Instead I take my bag
and leave you
shuffling the cards again,
hoping the draw
is in your favor
and wishing, too,
that the game
would never end.

Silver Brooch (In Memory of Dahlia)

You gave me a gift that day,
a silver brooch of leaves
and wrought flowers, with no precise
explanation.

I could not predict
your movements
as you raced
about, winding your way down
dark backroads
to unlikely destinations,
chasing past yourself
on impossible quests.

So when the package came
I could not have known
that it was time:
your search for shelter
behind glass walls,
beneath heavy cupboards,

was over.

No longer would you feel the pain
of the hunted, the fear of the sudden
hand reaching for your heart.

No more would angry voices
hiss out details of your destiny
as you hung tight between
your future
and your riddled past.

You had come to the decision
that was already made,
to let the chase move on
without you, to lie still
at last, after you had given
everything away.

What I'm Trying to Explain...

some wish
for diving under,
filling lungs with blackness
of water

shutting down
the counting machine,
endless duster, polisher, orderer
of things

things everywhere
wood, paper, steel,
sharp and hard and bent and cluttered—

a wish
for curving inward
blood and darkness,
screams that shatter
windows,
topple lists of things, things, things

then scream louder:
"I am the true sound.
Nothing else matters."

Sirens, Wednesday, Noon, 1963

She stops cold
in the doorway
as schoolmates' voices rise
and fall.

Leaves crack beneath
their careless feet
announcing
the impending frost.

She tastes the iron-grey
of the sky, digs
her nails
into her palms

and yearns for the past—
life before danger,
before speech,

when her mother's face

lit with joy
and sleep came softly
in her arms.

It is a memory she is not sure of.
But she clings
to its foggy edge
to ease the twisting of her heart,
the rumbling in her head,

as the weekly wailing starts,
prophesying the end
of the world.

Ultima

Our orchid is blooming now,
great with blossoms
tugging on their stem,
propped up by a thin green rod
that you placed there gently
so as not to disturb them.

Once I held
a small petal
inside me,
dared not jostle her
for fear she would vanish
in her transparency.

But I lost her
anyway.
They spread my legs
and scraped her dust
away as if she had not been
beautiful, had not been ours.

We grieved for her,
called her Ultima—
ultimate gift,
withdrawn.

We imagine her still,
reaching toward the sun,
tender toward children
captured by darkness,
extinguished by the cruelty
of night.

Grace (for Nicole)

She said the maple tree
reminded her
of Maine
as we sat by the lake
in Como.

There was fire
in her eyes
that flashed
as she spoke,
her words
a prayer sung
once, twice, three times,
again

as the autumn breeze
lifted her
to sights
she'd never seen
and her endless restless energy

left us
breathless.

I stirred my coffee
enviously,
wishing
for her grace,
until I heard a break
in her voice
and recognized
my name.

Embroidery

Mama, your eyes are black
with pain,
your fingers twisted
as you pass thread through
the needle
to stitch stiff patterns
on linen cloth.

Still, a tree appears,
loop by loop,
cross by cross,
and I bend to touch you

but you pull away,
piercing the skin
of your creation.

I see strangers
in your face,
changing
with the light:

one who lives with poison
in her veins,
one who softens
with old age,

and I wish I knew you.

Stitch by stitch, loop by loop
you build your world
of two dimensions,
then fold it into place
for safe keeping.

Partial Eclipse

Last night, through the clouds,
we saw the moon,
full of orange light,
glide across the sky.

Then, precisely at ten,
the earth spun before it,
shutting out the light.

Inside, candles burned.
Music floated up
as we sipped our wine
and danced from in to outside,
connecting everything:

Once, we lost a child
who didn't belong in this world.
Once, you sat by my bedside,
sick with fear.
Once, you almost left me,

but we survived.

If we knew a god
we would thank him
for holding our souls together,

just as ancient tribes
sang with deep relief
as the earth moved on
and moonlight reappeared.

Mirrors

Yesterday
a man and his wife
died ten minutes apart
in their nursing home in Leeds.

When they told him
she was gone
he slipped
into her bed
and gazed
at her mirrored
eyes
until he, too,
could no longer
see.

Then there was no breath,
no rustling
of sheets,
no sigh,
no weeping...

They must have been

in training
all their lives,

creating a secret
syntax
to embrace
their world.

They must have
planned it
this way

each morning
when they found themselves
waking
from similar
dreams,
beginning another day
of the miracle
no one could
believe.

When it Comes

When it comes
it comes in an instant.

All at once
the world is in
relief—trees and mountains
outlined
in black,
painful in their beauty,
sharp as broken
glass.

Words spin
inside me,
foreshadowing
the future

while anxious chords
and harmonies
revolve

in my head.

There is no rest
in this cruel
transformation—
crowds force their way
round me
staring deep
into my eyes until
I am naked.

I yearn for silence,
or oblivion,
but must endure
this cacophony
until it decides
to move
away.

Close Escape

Darkness is falling quickly
on the mountain lake
where we make our home

and I am in shadow,
swept up in shards of frost
without you.

The sun has not appeared
for days.
Eyes ache
for blessed light, held back
by tears
for the missing.

You have captured me whole.
My heart, my arms, my fingertips
are yours;

you are the one who

whisks me from falling,

clears my path
of broken glass.

I will never lose my fear
of losing you—
the scream that screams forever
and shakes me to the bone.

But when you return
I will push away
the soreness of the heavy night
and turn to kiss your hands,
your face with the grace
that comes of a close escape
from the razor's edge.

Taking Care of Things

There was the noise
of rockets falling
like stars from a child's sky.

There was the noise
of voices rising
voracious with my name.

There was the noise
of someone running
trying to scuttle them away.

There was the sound
of sounds repeating
sufferers screeching, high C's sharpening,
footsteps scraping

and when I turned
I noticed you there,
saying something simple

that jumped up, then
stood quietly to pacify the air.

In a Sculptor's Garden, St. Ives, Cornwall

I would like to dig
my spade
into this sandy soil
each morning
as the mist
fades

and the pale, gold light
butters the sky.

I would whiten
my hands
with the dust
of words
chiselled into curves
and angles,

scrape my arms
on points

that need
smoothing.

I would set
my lines
along the winding
paths

to nestle
among the bushes
and trees

and welcome
blazing summer,
unexpected
frost

with perfect contentment,
perfectly at peace.

Sunday

Today we stayed
indoors
and took the sun
through our
windows.

We curled
around each other
even as we went
our separate
ways

attending to this
and that.

Every fold
of cloth,
every scoured
pan
fit neatly

into place

as we measured out
the hours
by teaspoon,
careful not to drop
a single
grain.

The North Sea

We will walk
on a beach
by the North
Sea

wrapped in wool
and reflection

baring ourselves
to the chilly
sand

sharing
one voice

singing
with the sea
of other
incarnations.

We will not mind
the whipping
wind
for it will be
behind us

and we will only
stop
to marvel
as the sun
sinks
on the horizon.

Questions for my Mother

If I could see you now
I'd ask you

who sent you
crawling
on your knees,

bruising
your bones
as you scrubbed
yourself clean

only to begin
again?

Who made you
rip yourself
apart,

knit yourself

into a web
of yarn,

stuff your ears
with cotton?
I tried to speak
to you,
but you wandered off
in the eyes;

tried to reach
for you,
but you twirled
away.

I climbed
into bed
with you

when you were
dying,

and cried
for you,

for this was your final
suffering:

to stop short,
never
realizing
your torturer

was wrong.

When He Goes Away

When he goes away,
he hides himself
behind my pillow
so I can reach out
and touch his face,
crinkly with sleep,

and smell the night
on his chest
deeply breathing.

When he goes away,
I close my eyes
and hear him whisper,
music to my ears.

When he goes away,
I balance on a string
holding him tightly,
afraid to startle him

into space,
where I may not find him
until he returns.

Brother

I lay awake
often,
tuned to the whisper
of your breath
behind the wall,

wracked
with a vision
of cataclysm—
the prospect
of my loss.

How could I
protect you
from the darkness
that could spirit you
away?

How could I
save you

as you skipped
into the future
unclothed?

For I cherished
the curve
of the crown
of your head

sweet to the lips
of adoration.

I fed you
fantasies
that had sustained me,

milk blood
of my soul.

We were orphans
in the forest
of my mind

and I was

afraid,

for I could only
sing to you
with the wisdom
of a child.

Betrayal (In Memory of Ella)

It did not happen
right away.

When her news
came
he took her hand
as they sat
silent
by the kitchen
door.

But each day,
as she
weakened,
his sickness
spread

till his heart
turned black
and his head turned

against
the wall.

When he left,
she was twice
stricken.

He had betrayed
the body
that betrayed her

as if it were hers
alone.

Morning by the Lake

We lie,
the three of us,
in the deep shade
of a languorous
tree

protected
from a zealous
sun
and distant
perturbations.

The youngest
rests her head
in the crook
of her arm
and strokes
her fulsome
belly,

laughing
as the restless
child
tests the limits
of her womb.

When we are inspired
we walk
to the water's
edge

and navigate
a prickly path
among the pointed
stones

as we venture in.

Then we join
together,
three women

buoyed by the timeless
transformation

of mountain
snow,

basking
in the brilliant
imminence
of a cherished baby's
birth.

Heat Wave

It crept up
on us
till one day,
around noon,
the air closed in
like an elastic
band.

We walked
in slow, small
steps,
stopping
to catch
our breath

as the sun struck us
silly
and we searched
for relief.

It was all
we could talk about—
money and food,
joy and regret
were almost
forgotten

as we hid
in the paltry shade
of helpless
trees.

Maybe tomorrow...
though the forecasts
betrayed us.

Maybe it will rain...
We had to hold out
hope,

captives waiting for
a savior
to set us
free.

Then, one morning,
we awoke to a breeze.
It was not predicted,
not foreseen.
We spread our arms
and kicked up
our feet,
no longer at war
with our bodies.

Voices lifted
and rusty wheels
turned;
doors sprang open
to the sweet scent
of liberation

and we bent down
in praise
and quietly
colluded
to deny
that this gift

could quickly vanish
before our grateful eyes.

Heat Wave II

This is our space now—
this shuttered room
cooled by the whisper
of a whirring
fan.

You are not bothered.
You fill the space
with your imagination

like a child
beneath a blanket
strung across
two chairs.

Your lists
and dates
are scuttled

and you don't

care.

You are peacefully
suspended,
like heat above
the mountains

in no hurry
to move
on.

Reunion

How long
has it been
since we lay
side by side,
sister and brother,
on shaven grass,
giddy with the dew
of morning?
How long
since we followed
the wind—

you, the adventurer,
leading the way;
I, pedalling madly
to keep up
with your restless
soul?

Since you climbed

the stairs
of my rebellion
to reach your own

and, in the end,
far outstripped me?

It hardly matters now,
as we spot
each other
by the railway
gate

and a crush
of rushing memories
presses up
against our hearts.

The Last Kiss (In a Cemetery in Milan)

They struck you
bluntly,
deeply,
shockwaves
from chiselled
stone—

an eternal
grieving
as she bent
to cradle
her beloved.

Time had stopped
in mid-motion
and heartbreak rang
in your ears

thrumming
the swell

of your sadness

as your breath
quickened
and you ached
for the comfort
of an endless
embrace.

Nervous Breakdown

I was a puppet
in those days,

but no one laughed
when I fell
flat
on my face,

for I was not
entertaining.

My brittle legs
could not free me.

My brain was blunted
by a rain
of blows

and I was grieving.

People wondered
at the sudden
change.

Once I had entered rooms
fearlessly,

finding diamonds
in the shadows
of evening light.

Once I stroked
the subtle shapes
of words
and held them
to my lips

to taste
their stories.

For then I was not sealed
in silence.

I had not yet

held up my arms
in surrender

believing I was safe
at last
in the serpentine
embrace
of those
who would comfort me.

Fragments

In a box
under the stair
lived some pages
of my story.

I had not seen them
for years.

I approached them
blithely,

not suspecting words
emerging
from the past

once again
could smash me
into pieces

more invisible

than glass.

As I read,
I heard

their voices
as they pressed
my pain
into tidy
bundles;

felt their breath
as they leaned in
toward me,
hoping to measure
my heart.

I saw them
rush away
once they'd pronounced
my future

and though I knew better,
I fell deep

into fragments,

sharp as the pointed
finger
of remorse.

Madness (To Dr. L.)

In those days
I sang in strange tongues,
turned my skin inside out
without weeping.

I built dreams
of grandeur
out of sleepless nights
and raged at the sun
in the morning.

You came to me
as the wind rose.
I saw you
with the corner of my eye—
a blessing in disguise,
calling my name.

I read your eyes
for danger,

arching slowly
towards you,
preparing my escape.

But you were constant.
You did not frighten
me away.
You held me gently
as I whirled in place,

and waited patiently
for my redemption.

Observer

Each day at dawn
you wake
from dreams
of flying,

surveying scenes
of humbling
splendor

from breathless
heights.

You are still lost
in wonder

as you begin
your day—

struck by the cut
of your trousers,

the brilliance
of a broken
egg…

You do not rush
to destinations—

you move to the rhythm
of the music
that inspires you,

for each step
is a revelation,
a vivid
observation

caught complete
in the circle
of a moment,

round
as a colored
marble,
light as falling

snow.

You realize
your good fortune—

the gift
of the darkness
that long ago
embraced you,

threatened
to take you.

And you always
remember
how it kindly
set you free.

That Song

I had not heard
that song
for so long—

not since winter
dawns
far, far away,
when you'd gone
about your day

and I played it
loud and sang out
to the rising
sun
and the pale green
snowdrops born
of its light.

You had enthralled me,
your spell had

transformed me,
and I sang in praise

to the gods
of change, hoping

they could hear me,

knowing spells
can be whisked
away
with the sudden
wave
of a jealous
hand.

And I wept
for my past,
for my joy,
for my future

even as I danced
and raised my arms up
to the sky,

for the strange bliss
lifted me
and made me fly.

Wood Thrush

The thrush
is calling you

to the days
when you knew
its song—

when time
was not
splintered

and there was nothing
lost;

when the air
was not choked
with anger

and there was no
remorse;

when you thrived

in the fullness
of the forest

and found
the sound
of the sea.

Crossing Borders

It can be
distressing,
this shifting
ground—

things are not
where they were,

all markers
are torn
down.

I am losing
myself
in this place

of strange
dimensions,

inscrutable

laws,

for I can find
no center,

nowhere
to take
stock,

nowhere
to come back to

when I am
shattered
by my travels

and the building
fear
of earthquakes
of the heart.

Our Garden

I have planted
red impatiens
that look like
roses.

They drop
their blooms
like kisses
to a waiting
crowd

as we sit
in early evening
in the early days
of June.

The air
is kind
to us,
as we are

to each
other,

gently touching

our faces
with no threat,

no challenge.

This is our humble
garden—
moist soil cradling
the roots
of new life

bathed
in sun.

We are grateful
here
for it has become so
glorious
after all these years.

To Desiree

We walk
arm in arm
away
from the jarring
crowd

into this green
space

where fall
is turning
into winter.

We breathe in
the chill
of the dusky
air

and slowly
breathe out
our secrets.

We share the scars
of self-recrimination,
the twisting pain
of doubt,

though our wounds
were bound
in stories

that were
worlds apart.

Now, beneath
the heavy branches
of a shadowed
tree,

we bend gently
toward
each other

to exchange

gifts
of wisdom

like bits
of colored
glass
transformed
into treasures
by the restless
thrashing
of a careless sea.

I Am Not Myself Today

Today
I am not
myself.

I am stuck
in the viscous
gloom
of dreams

that threw me
down
into the hollow
underground

where everything I had
was missing.

I lay dazed
in pieces
on a chilly

floor,
caked in the dust
of seclusion,

as my fists
kept a rapid,
muted beat

and time
was blindly
passing.

I am not myself
today.
I can smell the fumes
of madness.

2 October

It must have rained
last night—

the roofs
below
have turned
a deeper gray

and clouds hang
damp
on the mountains.

Sunday's stillness
surrounds
me,
muffling

the sounds
of the shuffling
steps

of morning,

while you lie
bundled
in your dreams,

sheltered
from the brisk
October breeze,

clutching
my love
like a finger
in the tender
coil
of your hand.

To the End of Love (In Memory of Leonard Cohen)

Perhaps
it ends

when curtains
fray
and dark
cells

race
through gentle
veins;

when years
are lost
in tangles
of the mind

and her face
is the face

of a stranger.

Perhaps
it ends
like a wolf's
long
howl,

trailing off
into forbidding
skies.

Or perhaps
it goes
on—

light
as a whisper,

broad
as a master
plan,

reaching out

and folding
in

like the arms
of a lover

who had
been away

too long.

Birthday

My mother always
told me
that on the day
I was born

she saw the first
flowering
of a magnolia
tree.

This became our story,
shared as the warmth
of her womb,

and every birthday
we would carry it out
like a fine confection.

Still, each spring,
with the early

blossoming,
I can feel her heartbeat
quickening

as they lowered me
gently
into her tired
arms.

Russell Square Station, London (75 Years After the Blitz)

How many
have descended
here,
pushing
and squeezing
or simply weary
with flight?

How many
have walked
your well-worn
floors

anxiously waiting
or not afraid
at all?

I hear them
calling out
to mothers,
daughters,
lifelong

friends

in dim-lit
corridors
built to last.

I see the prints
of their fingers
on your green tiled
walls
as they reach out
in restless
sleep
or brush by
toward urgent
destinations.

There is always
the scramble
of bags
and feet
till late in the night,
when the roar
recedes
and your gates
are carefully
tended

and the memory
of refuge
flickers
like flames
that still
remain

after great
damage

is done.

The Painting Lesson

You put the brush
in my hand
just so

and guided me
through the petal
of a rose.

Your deftness
amazed me:

the steady swoop
of paint creating
light, creating
shadow.

Then you watched
as I tried
to reflect you,

desperately
grateful
for your kind
eyes
as you leaned
close,

smiling
your approval.

Long ago,
before the trouble
and the rage,

your smile sustained me
as you gathered me
in perfumed arms
and I stroked your love,
your beauty.

Long ago
you cherished me
and were my
queen.

And now,
in this new
universe,

you were again
the young mother,
washing sand
from my burning
eyes.

Pronto Soccorso (for Camilla)

She fell ill
in her own
darkness...

The pain came
like a demon
pounding
on her door

to shake her
from the restless
sleep

of the forsaken.

She was carried
away
by strangers

whose kindness
spoke to her
like music

from a distant
place

that she remembered
but had never
seen.

When they lifted her,
she was a dancer,

weightless as a rising
soul;

and when they gathered tightly
round her
to see what could be done,

the pain
was like a clock

ticking softly,

measuring the rhythm
of her abundant
heart.

After the Flu

This was an easy
illness.

It did not choke me
or turn me
into stone.

There were no demons
to crawl beneath
my skin,
refusing to be shaken
away.

It was not plagued
by weighty compounds
cruel as alchemy,
promising
gold.

No, this was entirely
different,

for it did not deface

me,
then leave me
all alone.

"The Moon is a Harsh Mistress"

I watch you
as the song
unfolds

like silk
finely woven
by a young
woman's
hands,

and your beauty
overcomes
me.

Her voice
spins
around you,

veils you
in the exquisite

pain

of love
lost
and hearts
fallen
from the brilliant
heights
of stars.

I dearly need
to hold you,

kiss the sorrow
from your eyes

though it is only
borrowed
from another

who did not share
the good
fortune

that is yours
and mine.

New York, 1963

Sometimes
on weekends
we would drive up
to Manhattan.

Our cousins
lived there
in a pre-war
apartment
with a doorman
in a cap
and an ice cream shop
next door.

I envied them
their wide, white rooms
with tall ceilings
and windows
with sills
you could sit on.

My aunt
had closets

filled with hats
and high-heeled
shoes
she would let me
try on

if she was in a
good mood.

My uncle
worked
in television
and knew important
people.

He did not know
how I loved him
and wished
I were my cousin
sitting on his knee.

At night
in my bed
in the servants' quarters
I would lie awake
listening to the constant
wail
of ambulances

and police cars

and my heart
would pound
and my stomach
tie in knots

when I realized
that if they dropped
the bomb

it would be here
in the center
of the world

where millions of people raced
on crowded streets

and some
lucky ones
lived
in apartments

you could
get lost in.

The Language of Sisters (for Genevieve)

For years
after you were
gone

I saw you flying
like Mercury,
seldom able
to set
down.

A scarf
thrown across
a chair;
a single can
of oysters
on a kitchen
shelf,

and you,
natural Empress,
waltzing
to the tune

of tolling
bells.

Now that we are older,
reunited,
we find we share the language
of sisters,

and we begin to build
ourselves
a shelter
with our remembered
words.

And from this place
we go out
together

as the music
of our voices
weaves us gently
through

the layers
of each other's
lives.

Mutual Creation

How lovely they are—
the blood-red pepper,
the onion and corn,
simmering in the pan,
like stained glass lit
by fire.

You throw back your head
and laugh
as you crack an egg
against the side
of a bowl
and watch it slide
to the bottom,

and I lean in towards you
to reach a wooden
spoon.

Seamlessly sharing steps
like seasoned dancers,

we are building something new
from disparate pieces,

chopping, mixing, spreading
till it rises
to become itself—

our mutual creation.

Heat Wave, London

Remember that day
we danced in the fountain
in the park,
water rushing round
our grateful feet,
brushing up
against our thighs?

We laughed
into the searing sun,
the grass bleached
and overgrown
as a savannah,

and we both remarked
on our good fortune.

The night before,
you disobeyed
yourself

and cried out
the struggle

you'd been hiding.

It seemed as though
the friend I knew
was trapped inside
parentheses
of pain,

a subset
of a self
suffused
with suffering.

But in the morning,
as we laughed
and danced
and the marble
felt cool on our feet,

I saw you kick aside
your grief

like errant stones
and leaves
caught up
on a blistering day
in the blissful flow
of a welcome
fountain.

I Remember This:

Cool girls
huddled
in the lunchroom,
proud of new
nylon stockings,
breasts budding
in pointed
bras,
savouring tales
of blood
and danger
and the pure,
delicious pleasure
of being members
of this club.

Now they talk
of children
having children,
displaying polished
memories
of their own proud
pregnancies

like family
jewels
that sparkle
with the charge
of expectation,
held high above
the common
concerns
of the quotidian

and beyond me,
as I stand apart
feeling parched
as a corner plot
where nothing
grows.

Ultima II

I still think
of you,
my sweet one,
my ultimate
child,

for you
wander
within me

and you are all
around.

I hear your heart
beat
in seconds
passing...

your breath
weaves round
and tangles
with mine

till I can't tell
who's breathing.

It was long ago
when I carried you
in darkness
and had to let you
go.

Your tissue
skin
could not contain you;

you did not intend
to wait for me
to urge you
toward
the light.

But then
I named you

and you filled the
name

with faceless
beauty

and the ululating
cry

of broken
promise

and unrequited
love.

Summer Memory

We lay back
on the tall
grass,
its points
prickling
our naked
thighs,

the sun
blazing
on our half-closed
eyes,

the clicks
and cries
of bugs
and birds

lulling us
further

into a languor

that made our heads
swim
and our arms
and legs
heavy
as sacks
of stones.

Nearby,
a wooden
rowboat
stirred
the lake

and in its wake,
lithesome
waves slipped
onto
the shore.

We spread our warm arms
out

beside us,

relishing
an errant
breeze

and breathing in
the yellow-green
of the meadow
with its slight

scent
of hay,

feeling ourselves
fall
deep
into our own
impressions

in the
sweet,
tall
grass.

Too Long

It's been so long
since we walked
in the dazzle
of pale purple leaves
freshly fallen,

not daring to speak,
but listening to the breath
of trees listening
to each other.

It's been too long
since we were whipped
by frenzied snow,
dazed by its luminous
omnipresence,
losing ourselves
in the pathless expanse
of earth and sky.

Dying Girl

She lifted
the girl
who was dying

onto her shoulders
and brought her
to a bright lawn
still damp
with early morning
rain

and lay with her
on the plush green
ground

and said, with her eyes
and her kind arms and kisses
on the young girl's
cheeks,

"Let me take your pain
in my hands
and turn it into silver rings

that we can put
on our fingers.

"We will be linked
like lovers,
at ease with each other,
with casual embrace.

"I promise to hear you always,
and to see your face,
and you can take me with you,
even into places
beyond imagining."

Then they leaned together
and closed their eyes,
exchanging the gifts
of a lifetime,
one by one.

Visiting Philadelphia

This time it was different.

I settled in
without a bump,
without the shock
of landing.

I took right to the streets,
sure in my direction,
always knowing what to say,
even without
thinking.

Old friends and I
skipped
Double Dutch
through time

revealing splendid interwoven
cords

we had all but forgotten.

In the end
I could have stood comfortably
among a row
of houses
and not stood out—

my shutters as old
and blue
as all the rest,

not needing to be
anything
else.

Box of Stone (for Ginger)

You stand
by the factory's broken
window
in a drizzling
rain

hearing the phantom
roar
of a thousand
women
working,

remembering
your sister
returning home
after bitter days,
fresh coins
in her pockets...

She would buy you

things
that dreams were made of:
fragrant, dark-eyed dolls,
dresses bright
with the silver
lining
of clouds,

as she planned
her own escape.

As time contracts
and your body
fails you

you reach back
and prick yourself
on the poison
of your past,

which you cannot
let go—

you clamp it

to your chest
though it is rife
with evil;

you encase it
in a box of stone
that you will carry
with you

wherever you go.

You will stand
beneath
the window
in the pouring
rain

and turn your back
against your future

till it bolts up
and whispers
your name.

Winter Voyage

When the train
glides
past the border,

I lean my head
on the woolly
curve
of your shoulder

and bleached swaths
of sunlight
wrap us
in weightless warmth

we wish could last
forever.

We have closed our eyes,
but I'm not sleeping.

It is enough
to feel your breathing,

imagine the brilliant
colors
of your dreams.

Thermal Baths

We step in slowly,
lowering our bodies
down,
dazed
by the silvery
surface, squinting
in the wintry
sun.

As plumes of steam
rise around us,
we lean back
on the smooth
tile
rim
and feel our heads
spinning
slightly

as if we were dreaming
of flying,

weaving through white

clouds,

the sky's silky
silence,

aware of the wavy
flutter
of each other's
wings.

Little Theater (to Adina)

In the mirror
on your closet
door

we'd scrutinize
our pantomimes
of deep
emotion,

costumed
in the skins
of mysterious
adulthood,

complicit
in the drama
of our imagined
lives.

We were a fine
pair, both bearing
the bruises
of our fathers'
burdens,

which we never thought
to share.

Instead we danced
a dance
of our own
creation,

vaguely dreaming
that the world
would receive us
with awestruck
applause.

Early Morning

I wait for you
to wake,
to hear your steps
precede you,
coming towards me,
down the hall

and imagine you
in bed
behind the wall,
dreaming
of hippopotami
whose feet sound like
hands
beating on the smooth,
fragrant skins
of tabla;

imagine you sitting
by me

so close that I can smell
the scent
of your soul;

see you draw away
from me
like a reluctant
breeze

to fix sweet, milky
tea
to soothe me.

I wait to see you
patiently,
expectant as a pilgrim
who would climb
on her ageing knees
for the one
she loves.

Evening with an Old Friend (for Tony)

We sit
late into the night,
long after others
have gone,

charged
by memories
that crackle
between us

and fill us
with light.

Our words spill
into each other,
blending like the colors
of sunset,
fevered like the blush
of a dawning
sky.

I am suddenly
clear
in the mirror
of your eyes

and I see
the past,
now cast
in three dimensions,

where we sang
and danced
like wild men
through the tangles
of our minds.

There is no replacing
you, my friend.
Our lives have been braided
together
and now are linked more tightly
still

as we throw back

our heads
in swelling
laughter,
each wave building
on the other,
reaching, reaching up
to breathless
heights.

Memoir

Tonight,
while you are
sleeping,

I slip away
Into my Bad Old
Days,

and call them up
before me.

I do not intend
to undo them

or smooth their rough
edges
away—

just to see them
again

and search
to find words

for their extremity.

Some strike me
sideways,

leave me
reeling.

For though I know
they are there,
I don't see them
coming.

I had almost
forgotten
how it felt

that day
when all was lost
and the air
tasted

like iron

and I walked
half-naked
through the snow.

I had almost
forgotten

the panic
in my father's
eyes

as he tried
to strangle
my pain,

then locked
the door
behind
him.

I had almost
forgotten

the texture

of those days,

gritty
as ash,

steely
as a razor
blade,

and how it never
really occurred
to me

that they would ever
end.

Old Soldier

How sweet he seems
as he lays the wreath
of poppies
on the simple
grave.

"There are no words,"
he says, to those
who ask,
and he hides
his melting
face
in his hands.

He has never stopped
loving them—
the long-lost,
the lads as innocent
as he.

But it is only now
that he allows
this revelation

to fill his eyes
and tremble
in his voice—

only now,
when all his tasks
are done
and he has set
his affairs
in order,

does he dare
unseal
himself,

revealing
the man

he might
have been.

Orchids

They have become
so splendid
in your care.

Relentlessly
they reach
and climb
as if to wrest
their young
white flowers
from the earthy
tangles
of birth...

and you, most of all,
understand them.

When they are through,
they hide their urges
deep

inside themselves,

but you, unlike some,
don't forget them.

You have heard
that they prefer
that one
not touch them,

so your fingers hover
above them,

though you would love
to stroke them—

for you know
how they return
to you

unfailingly,

flushed
with restless energy

beneath
the reassurance

of your open hand.

Resolution, New Year's Day, 2017

I am tidying
my life
with soap
and steaming
water,

rubbing
my fingers
raw,

for I have lately
discovered

detail's
divinity

to rail
against
the shadows
of the passing

of time.

It is far
from easy:

daylight
is dim
and does not
last
long—

I strain
to see
the needle

that stitches up
my pieces

and makes me
whole.

But for now
I am determined
to sweep

and to sew

and to cleanse
myself
free

of the ashen
dread
of uncertainty.

About the Author

Jill Haber Pallone was born in Philadelphia in the USA, the daughter of a professor of engineering and an artist/art teacher. She studied English at the University of Pennsylvania, where she earned her undergraduate and graduate degrees. At Penn she was a student of the poet, William Jay Smith, and novelist Philip Roth, with whom she maintained a lifelong friendship. She has been a writer all her life, having published in such journals as the *Pennsylvania Review, Florida Quarterly, and Patterson Literary Review.* She most recently wrote a remembrance of Philip Roth for the *Pennsylvania Gazette* magazine. This is her first book of poetry.

Jill lives in Lugano, Switzerland, with her husband of more than three decades, Robert L. Pallone.

For more on Jill's poetry, including updates and new poems, please follow her on the Facebook page "Jill Pallone Poetry."